To Hear the Angels Sing

A Christmas Poem

BY W. NIKOLA-LISA

ILLUSTRATED BY JILL WEBER

Holiday House / New York

To my mother, who taught me to sing
W. N.

To Frank and Remy
J. W.

Text copyright © 2002 by W. Nikola-Lisa
Illustrations copyright © 2002 by Jill Weber
All Rights Reserved
Printed in the United States of America
The text typeface is ITC Tapioca.
The artwork was painted with acrylics and
acrylic based watercolors.
www.holidayhouse.com
First Edition

Library of Congress Cataloging-in-Publication Data
Nikola-Lisa, W.
To hear the angels sing: a Christmas poem / by W. Nikola-Lisa; illustrated by Jill Weber.
p.   cm.
Summary: A simple rhymed retelling of the Nativity story.
ISBN 0-8234-1627-5 (hardcover)
1. Jesus Christ—Nativity—Juvenile literature.
[1. Jesus Christ—Nativity] I. Weber, Jill, ill. II. Title.
BT315.2.N55 2002
232.92—dc21
2001039305

It came to pass
that Mary gave birth
to the Son of God...

She gave Him birth in Bethlehem,
Bethlehem, Bethlehem.
She gave Him birth in Bethlehem,
among the hay and sod.

The cows did low, the donkeys brayed,
donkeys brayed, donkeys brayed.
The cows did low, the donkeys brayed,
a shepherd blew his horn.

And Joseph bowed his head and prayed,
head and prayed, head and prayed.
And Joseph bowed his head and prayed,
when Christ the Lord was born.

A brightly shining evening star,
evening star, evening star.
A brightly shining evening star
shone boldly through the night.

Three wise men followed from afar,
from afar, from afar.
Three wise men followed from afar
the brightly burning light.

With gifts that only kings bestow,
kings bestow, kings bestow.
With gifts that only kings bestow,
they gave to Him gladly.

The blessed infant turned and waved,
turned and waved, turned and waved.
The blessed infant turned and waved,
glad tidings He did give.

The kings did bow, then went away,
went away, went away.
The kings did bow, then went away
to spread the word, He lives.

And people came from far and wide,
far and wide, far and wide.
And people came from far and wide
to see the King of Kings.

They came to be close by His side,
by His side, by His side.
They came to be close by His side
to hear the angels sing.

Behold the joy of Bethlehem,
     Bethlehem, Bethlehem.
Behold the joy of Bethlehem
     on this first Christmas morn.

When in this land of Abraham,
Abraham, Abraham.
When in this land of Abraham,

Christ the Lord was born.